Chance, Statistics and Graphs

World Teachers Press

Published with the permission of R.I.C. Publications Pty. Ltd.

Copyright © 1996 by Didax, Inc., Rowley, MA 01969. All rights reserved.

First published by R.I.C. Publications Pty. Ltd., Perth, Western Australia.

Printed in the United States of America.

Order Number 2-5010
ISBN 1-885111-22-3

A B C D E F 96 97 98 99

395 Main Street
Rowley, MA 01969

Introduction

Chance and statistics play an important part in today's society. People are placed in chance situations all the time and meet statistics wherever they turn. This book is designed to give students a relative and practical introduction into these two areas of mathematics.

Objectives: Grades 1-3

Pages	6 to 9	Play games based on chance
Pages	10 to 20	Use chance to generate number facts and provide data for discussion and recording
Pages	21 to 35	Collect, read and interpret samples of information and graph data
Pages	36 to 39	Blank Graph Masters - design your own activity

Contents

Teacher Information

Introduction

Chance and statistics play an important part in today's society. Increasingly, statistics play an important part in our lives as we collect data and analyze it in the quest to improve. The learning of these areas of mathematics is both challenging and fun. Activities can be structured to deal with well-known everyday topics as well as use motivating materials.

All activities have been based on experiences familiar to students. Each activity can be extended to provide more difficult situations or problems.

Remember the old problem:
If I tossed a coin ten times and it came up 'heads' each time, what are the chances that the next toss will be a 'head'?

What are the students' responses to this question?

Chance

Chance is based on the concept that there are many different possibilities that exist for a given action, e.g. the rolling of dice. This concept is developed by the understanding, through a variety of activities, of how different possibilities are achieved. The greater variety of activities that is provided, the greater the chances of understanding.

Statistics

The area of *Statistics* centers around the organized collection of data from a given activity or action. Unorganized data is simply data, however, once organized this data becomes statistics. Activities in this section of the book center on organizing data as it is collected so that the final product represents easily understood statistics.

Graphs

Graphing is a way of representing statistics. It is the process of taking collected data and representing it in a pictorial form. Graphs range from the simple to the very complex, however, the main purpose is to present information in a format that will assist with the interpretation of data.

You can design your own graphing activities for your students using the graphing forms on pages 36-39.

Teacher Information - Example Lesson Development

The following is a lesson development using one of the pages in this book. It is an example of how the activity could be introduced, developed and extended.

Activity   Amazing Dice: page 6

Introductory Work

This activity is developing the concept of Chance. Therefore discussion should center on what we mean by chance - the possibility that a certain action will occur. To reinforce this understanding apply the word 'chance' to the day-to-day activities of the students. For example, what is the chance that it will rain tomorrow? What is the chance that it will be hot tomorrow? What is the chance that someone in our class will be absent this week? Dice are used extensively in chance activities as they are a medium that offers multiple possibilities for the one action. The number of dice will extend this even further. It is recommended that a 'play' period be used before beginning dice activities so that the initial excitement of playing with the dice will not interrupt the purpose of the activities.

Completing the Worksheets

The following is a suggestion for the development and extension of this activity.

1. It is important that students understand how to play the game. Have the group play the first two moves with the class so that the teacher can identify any misunderstanding.

2. Use colored counters to mark the positions of each student.

3. Students should play the game several times to reinforce their understanding of chance.

4. Discuss with the whole class the problems they encountered. This will enable you to further reinforce the concept of chance.

Note: Enlarging the activity sheet may assist younger students.

Extension

The extension of the game is to vary the numbers that are used and also to increase the number of dice.

Amazing Dice

Name _____

With a partner, throw a die. Move only if you throw a 1, 3 or 6. Then move that number of spaces.
Try to find your way through to the end of the maze and win.

Start

Finish

0's and X's

Throw a die to move around the board. If you land on a **0**, move ahead two spaces. If you land on a **X**, move back two spaces. Can you beat your partner?

Start

	0	0		X		

Finish

	X	X	X	

	0		0		X
		0	X	0
		X		X
0	X		
0			

Square Maze

Name _____

With a partner, throw a die. Move ahead one square for each number you throw. If you land on a square that has an 'X' in it move back one square. If you land on a square that has an 'O' in it take another turn. The winner is the first one through the maze.

Start　　　　　　　　　　　　　　　　　**Finish**

Square Spiral

Name _____

Throw two dice and move ahead the number of squares you throw.
You win the game if you are the first to reach the middle square.

If you land on a:

- ❤ Move ahead 6 spaces
- ✔ Move ahead 2 spaces
- ✖ Move back 2 spaces
- ✳ Move ahead 12 spaces
- ✌ Go back to the beginning

Start

Colored Squares

With a partner, throw a die. If you throw more than a three, color in a square. After five minutes, count the squares each person has colored. The winner is the person who has colored the most squares.

Square Lines

With a partner, throw a die. If you throw less than a four, color in a square. The winner is the first person to make a line of six squares going across or down the page.

Circle Maze

Throw a die with your partner and see who can find a way into the circle maze first. If you land on a black square, go ahead an extra two spaces.

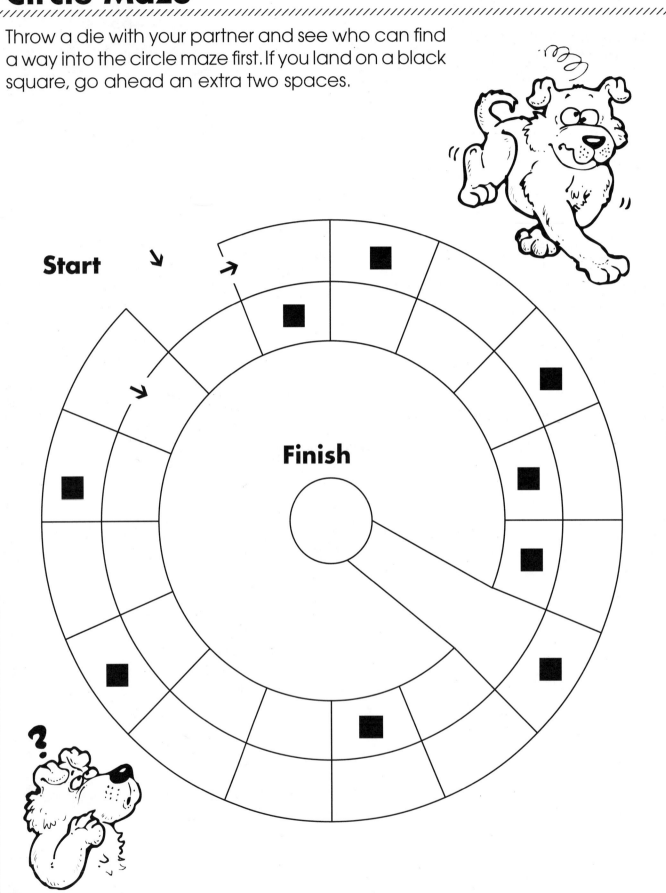

Start

Finish

World Teachers Press   *Chance, Statistics and Graphs, Grades 1-3*

Counter Target

Name _____

Throw a counter onto the target five times.
Add up the total score.
If the counter crosses a line, count the larger number.

What is the highest score you could get? _____

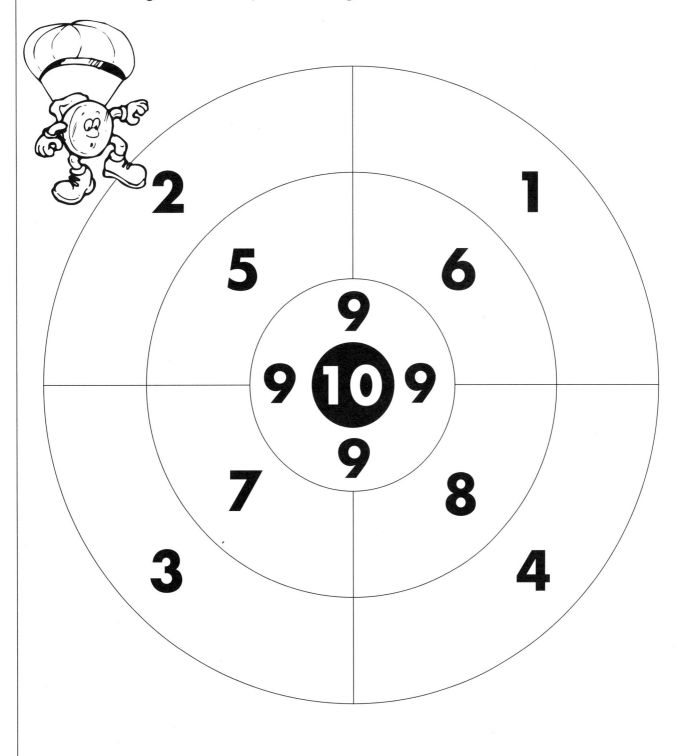

Dice Target

Name _____

Throw two dice and add the numbers. You must try to throw the numbers 2, 3, 4, 5, 6, 7, 8, 9, 10, 11 or 12. When you throw any of these numbers, color in a part of your target. But, you can only use a number once!

How many throws did it take you to color in the whole target? _____

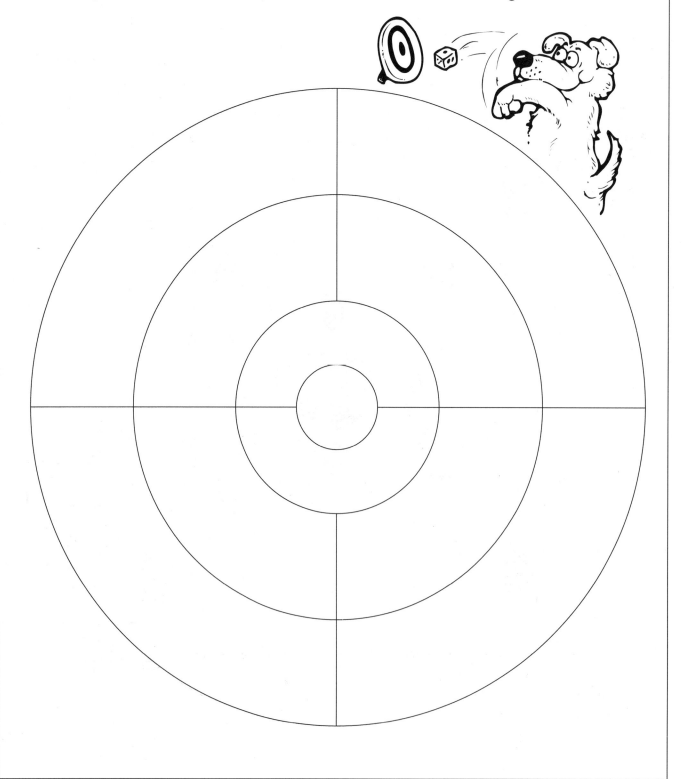

Dice Numbers

Throw a die.
Color in a box under the number you throw.
Do this forty times.

1	2	3	4	5	6

Which number was thrown most often? _____
Compare with a friend.

Two Dice

Throw two dice and add them together.

What is the total? _____

Do this twenty times.
Color in a matching square for each answer.

2	3	4	5	6	7	8	9	10	11	12

Which number was thrown most often? _____

Can you explain why? _____

Domino Pick Up

Name _____

Pick up ten dominoes, one at a time, from a pack.
Color in a matching box for each number on the
domino each time you pick up a number.

Which number came up most often? _____

0	1	2	3	4	5	6

Try this activity several times.
Did the same thing happen each time? _____

_____

Lucky Squares

You will need two dice. Mark one of them with a 1 and the other with a 2. Throw them and find the square in the table that shows the two numbers. Color in that square. Let your partner do the same. Once a square has been colored in, it may not be used again. The winner is the person who colors in the most squares.

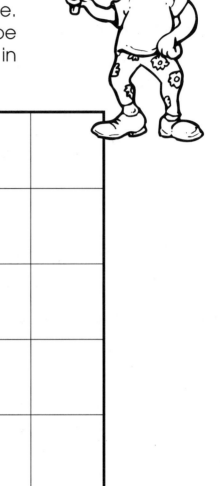

Die 2

1
2
3
4
5
6

1   2   3   4   5   6

Die 1

Which squares were colored in first? _____

Which squares were the last to be colored in? _____

Is there a reason for this? _____

_____

Dice Multiplication

- With a partner, throw two dice.
- Multiply the numbers on the dice and color the matching square.
- Once a square has been colored, it cannot be used again.
- When all the squares have been colored in, the winner is the person who has colored in the greatest number of squares.

15	20	12	10	9	8
18	25	24	20	18	16
30	30	36	30	36	36
18	25	24	20	18	16
15	20	12	10	9	8
6	5	4	3	2	1

Which numbers came up most often? _____

Is there a reason for this? _____

_____

Which numbers were hardest to throw? _____

Is there a reason for this? _____

_____

A Race to 96

Name _____

- With a friend, see how quickly you can move around the board.
- Throw two dice and find their total.
- Move ahead that many spaces.
- If you throw a double, you can move twice that distance.
- If you throw a double one, you can also have another turn or move ahead six extra spaces.

1	2	3	4	5	6	7	8	9
								10
19	18	17	16	15	14	13	12	11
20	21	22	23	24	25	26	27	28
								29
38	37	36	35	34	33	32	31	30
39	40	41	42	43	44	45	46	47
								48
57	56	55	54	53	52	51	50	49
58	59	60	61	62	63	64	65	66
								67
76	75	74	73	72	71	70	69	68
77	78	79	80	81	82	83	84	85
								86
95	94	93	92	91	90	89	88	87

96

Try this game again, but this time make up your own rules.

What are the new rules?

_____
_____
_____
_____
_____
_____
_____
_____
_____
_____

Pet Colors

Name _____

What colors are the pets belonging to the students in your class? Color in a box for each pet's color. Some students may have more than one pet, or a pet may be more than one color.

White

Black

Brown

Green

Yellow

Red

Blue

Orange

Which color is most common? _____

Hair Colors

How many students in your class have:

blond hair? [ ]   **black hair?** [ ]

brown hair? [ ]   **red hair?** [ ]

Color the boxes below to show the answers.
Each box shows one student's hair color.

Blond   **Brown**   **Black**   **Red**

Eye Colors

How many students in your class have:

blue eyes?

green eyes?

brown eyes?

other colors?

Color the boxes below to show the answers.
Each box shows one student's eye color.

Blue　　　　**Brown**　　　　**Green**　　　　**Other**

Car Colors

What color is your family's car/cars?

Ask the students in your class what color their families' car/cars are.

Color	Tally	Total
white		
red		
blue		
green		
yellow		
brown		
orange		
pink		
gray		
black		
cream		
silver		
gold		
other		

Which was the most popular color? _____

Is there a reason for this? _____

_____

Months and Height

Name _____

Measure your height in inches at the end of every month and graph your results.

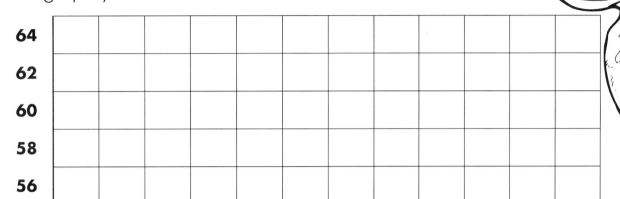

	Sept.	Oct.	Nov.	Dec.	Jan.	Feb.	Mar.	April	May	June	July	Aug.
64												
62												
60												
58												
56												
54												
52												
50												
48												
46												
44												
42												
40												
38												
36												
34												
32												
30												

In which month did you grow the most? _____

How much did you grow during the year? _____

Birthdays

Name _____

Graph the number of students born in each month of the year in your class.

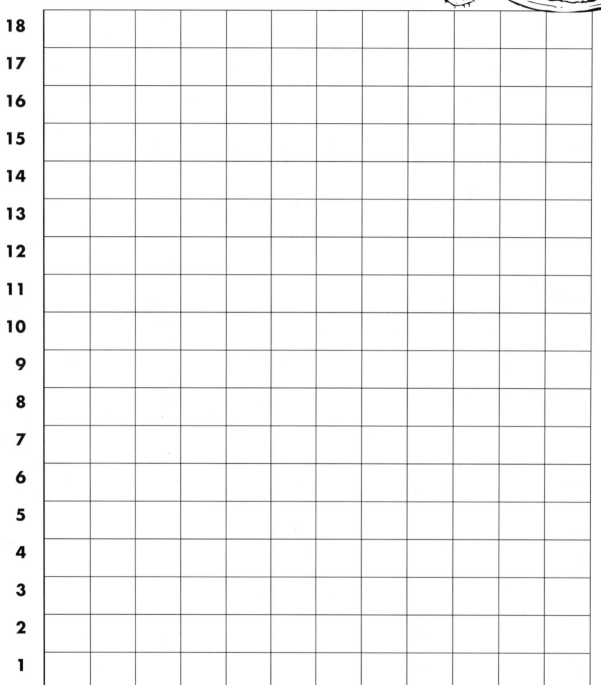

	Sept.	Oct.	Nov.	Dec.	Jan.	Feb.	Mar.	April	May	June	July	Aug.
18												
17												
16												
15												
14												
13												
12												
11												
10												
9												
8												
7												
6												
5												
4												
3												
2												
1												

Which month has the greatest number of birthdays?_____

 World Teachers Press *Chance, Statistics and Graphs, Grades 1-3*

House Numbers

What is your house number? ☐

What are the house numbers of the six students in your group?

Name _____ house number ☐

Name _____ house number ☐

Name _____ house number ☐

Name _____ house number ☐

Name _____ house number ☐

Name _____ house number ☐

Answer these questions.

1. Which digit is used most? _____

2. Which digit is used least? _____

3. What is the largest house number? _____

4. What is the smallest house number? _____

5. How many '1s' are there in all the house numbers? _____

6. Take the smallest house number from the largest.

   What is the difference? _____

7. Are there any consecutive house numbers? _____

Pets

Name _____

Below is a bar graph that shows the number of pets the students in Sunny Beach 3rd Grade class have. Can you answer the questions below?

Pet Numbers

Legend:
- ■ Dogs
- Mice
- Cats
- Birds
- Rabbits
- Fish

Which animal is the most popular pet? _____

Which animal is the least popular pet? _____

How many animals are owned by the class? _____

Put the pets in order from most popular to least popular.

_____

_____

How many dogs and cats are there? _____

How many birds and rabbits are there? _____

Absent

Below is a graph that shows the number of students absent in the first six months of a second grade class at Sunny Beach School. Answer the questions below.

Children Absent

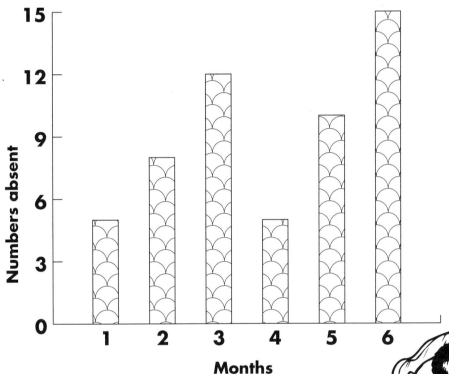

1. **September**
2. **October**
3. **November**
4. **December**
5. **January**
6. **February**

Which two months had the lowest number of students absent?

_____

_____

In which month were the most students absent? _____

How many days were the students absent altogether? _____

How many students have been absent in your class this month? _____

How many were absent last month? _____

Favorite Cakes

Below is a **PIE GRAPH** showing students' favorite cakes.
Can you answer the questions below?

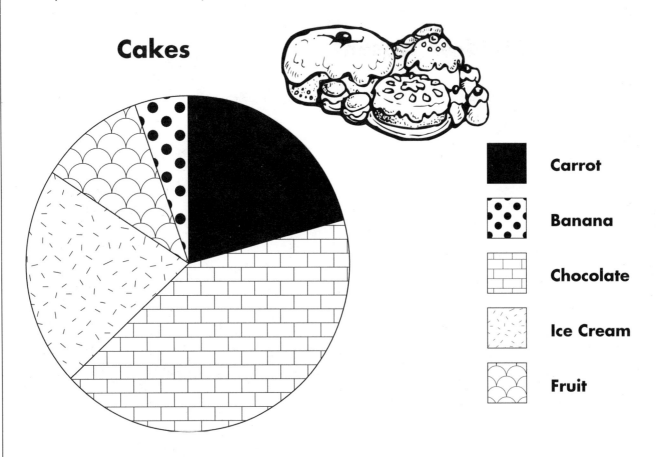

Cakes

■ **Carrot**

▣ **Banana**

▤ **Chocolate**

▦ **Ice Cream**

▧ **Fruit**

Which is the most popular type of cake? _____

Which is the least popular cake? _____

Order the cakes from most popular to least popular. _____

_____

_____

Why do you think this type of graph is called a 'pie' graph?

_____

_____

Sally's Piggy Bank

Name _____

Sally opened her Piggy Bank and found the following coins in it.
Answer the questions about her money graph.

Sally's Piggy Bank

Which coin did Sally have the least of? _____

How much were the 10¢ coins worth? _____

How much were the 50¢ and $1 coins worth altogether? _____

How many coins did Sally have in her piggy bank? _____

Which group of coins is worth the most? _____

How much were the 1¢ coins worth? _____

How much money was in the piggy bank altogether? _____

Bouncing

Name _____

Seven students had a ball bouncing contest. They had to see how many times they could bounce a basketball in twenty seconds. The results are shown in the graph.

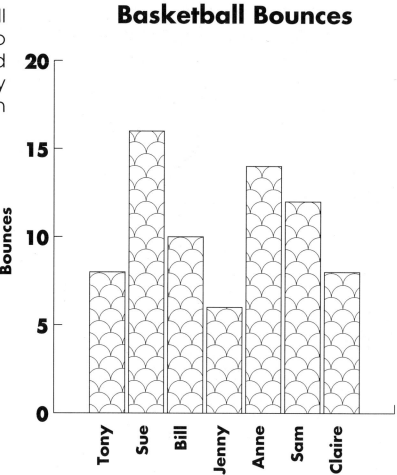

Basketball Bounces

Who won the contest? _____

Who came last? _____

What was the difference between the winning and losing score? _____

How many more bounces did Anne have compared to Claire? _____

How many bounces did Anne, Sam, Jenny and Tony have altogether? _____

How many bounces were there in the contest altogether? _____

If the contest went for forty seconds, what do you think the results may have been?

_____

_____

World Teachers Press   *Chance, Statistics and Graphs, Grades 1-3*

Marbles

Sue and Ian decided to put their marble collection together. Below is the table they drew up to find out what type of marbles they had.

Marble	Tally	Total
Red	IIII IIII IIII II	**17**
Green	IIII IIII I	**11**
Brown	IIII III	**8**
Yellow	IIII IIII IIII IIII	**20**
Pink	IIII	**5**
Orange	IIII IIII I	**11**
Clear	IIII IIII IIII	**15**

Of which type of marble do they have most? _____

How many more orange and clear marbles are there than yellow and pink?

_____

How many marbles are there altogether in their collection? _____

If Ian put in forty marbles, how many did Sue put in? _____

Which two marbles have the same total? _____

On the next page you will need to make a graph of the information in the table above. A grid and starting points will be given.

Name _____

Sue and Ian's Marble Collection

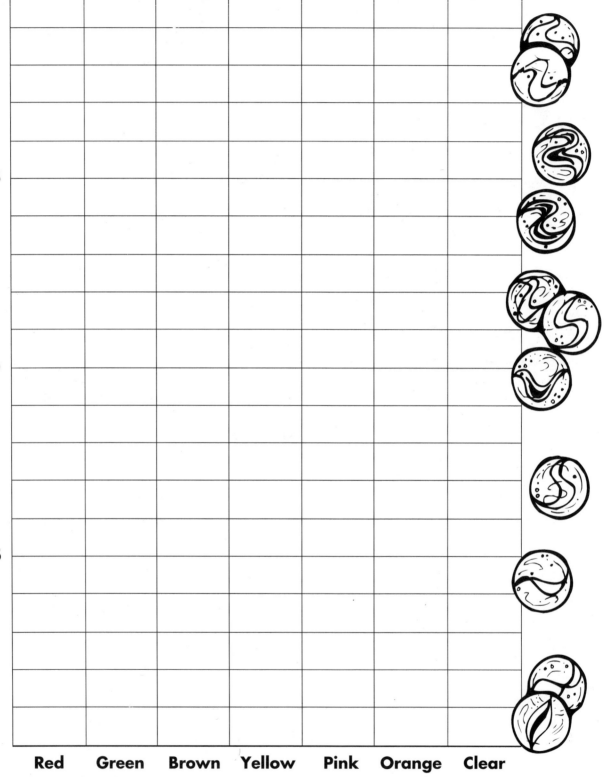

Number of Marbles (y-axis, marked 5, 10, 15, 20)

Red   Green   Brown   Yellow   Pink   Orange   Clear

Television

Ask your classmates about any seven television programs, to find out which of them is the most popular. Tally the information and graph your results.

Show	Tally	Total
1.		
2.		
3.		
4.		
5.		
6.		
7.		

	Show 1	Show 2	Show 3	Show 4	Show 5	Show 6	Show 7
24							
23							
22							
21							
20							
19							
18							
17							
16							
15							
14							
13							
12							
11							
10							
9							
8							
7							
6							
5							
4							
3							
2							
1							

Bar Graph Master 1

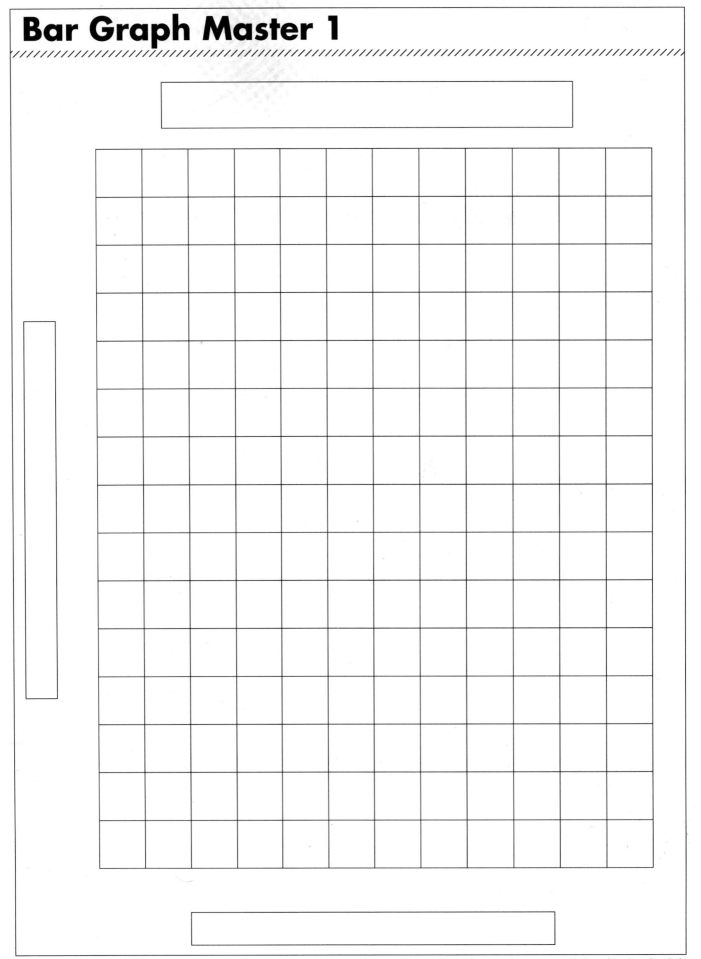

World Teachers Press *Chance, Statistics and Graphs, Grades 1-3*

Bar Graph Master 2

Graph Master 3

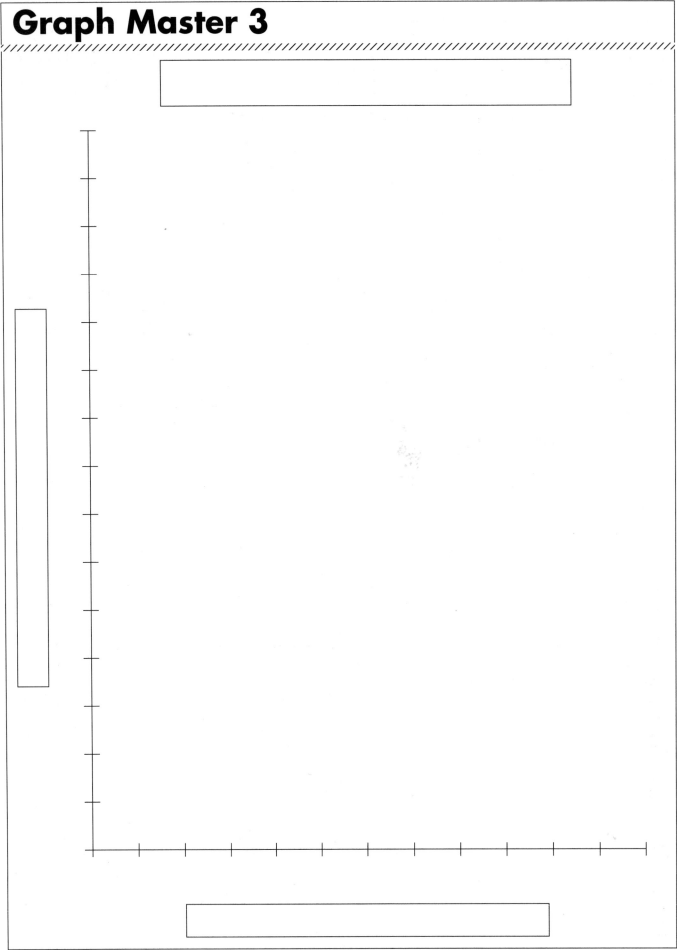

Graph Master 4

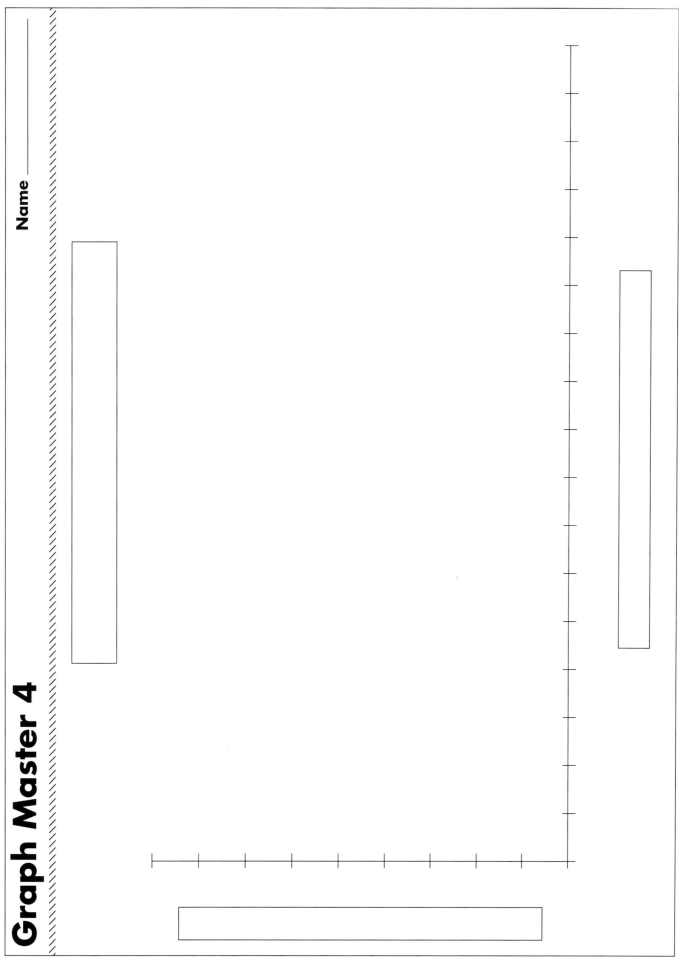

About the Author

Rik Carter, Perth, Western Australia.

Rik has over 15 years experience in Australian primary schools as a classroom teacher, schools advisory teacher and administrator. He has a special interest in mathematics and has used his classroom and advisory experience to produce a range of titles for primary schools.